Animal Bedtime

Jennifer Bové

muddy boots™

we jump in puddles

Guilford, Connecticut

Published by Muddy Boots
An imprint of Globe Pequot
MuddyBootsBooks.com

Distributed by NATIONAL BOOK NETWORK

The National Wildlife Federation © 2017 All rights reserved

Book design by Katie Jennings Campbell

Front cover photo © iStock.com/JohnCarnernolla, back cover photo and page 12 © iStock.com/epantha, title page and page 27 © iStock.com/kugelblitz, table of contents and page 11 © iStock.com/Tuomas_Lehtinen, page 2 © iStock.com/Schaef1, page 4 © iStock.com/Peter ten Broecke, page 7 © iStock.com/CharlieMlllerKB, page 8 © iStock.com/moisseyev, page 9 © iStock.com/Peeraphont, page 13 © iStock.com/Terryfic3D, page 14 © iStock.com/Tihis, page 16 © iStock.com/mildhightraveler, page 17 © iStock.com/krithnarong, page 18 © iStock.com/400tmax, page 19 © iStock.com/TommL, page 20 © iStock.com/halbrindley, page 22 © iStock.com/satit_srihin, page 23 © iStock.com/asxsoonxas, page 24 © iStock.com/ivz, page 26 © iStock.com/KenCanning, page 28 © iStock.com/Prig-Studio, page 29 © iStock.com/SWKrulllmaging.

The National Wildlife Federation & Ranger Rick contributors: Children's Publication Staff, Licensing Staff including Deana Duffek, Michael Morris & Kristen Ferriere, and the National Wildlife Federation in-house naturalist David Mizejewski

Thank you for joining the National Wildlife Federation and Muddy Boots in preserving endangered animals and protecting vital wildlife habits. The National Wildlife is a voice for wildlife protection, dedicated to preserving America's outdoor traditions and inspiring generations of conservationists.

British Library Cataloguing-in-Publication Information available

Library of Congress Cataloguing in Publication Data available

ISBN 978-1-63076-290-2 (paperback)
ISBN 978-1-63076-291-9 (e-book)

∞™ The paper used in this publication meets the minimum requirements of American National Standard for Information Sciences—Permanence of Paper for Printed Library Materials, ANSI/NISO Z39.48-1992.

Printed in the United States of America

Contents

Yawn! This fox is sleepy.

Animals get tired,
just like people do.
But animals don't
sleep in beds.
Let's find out where
animals like to doze.

A leopard lounges on a limb.

A sleeping
sloth hangs
from a branch.

A koala is cozy in
the crook of a tree.

A bear snoozes
on a bed of moss.

These fawns fell asleep
in a grassy field and
on a gravel path.

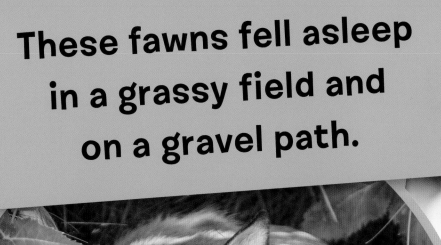

A hedgehog
curls up tight
to sleep.

River otters cuddle for a nap.

A meerkat family cuddles close together at bedtime.

Walruses pile up on the seashore to snore.

Bats sleep hanging upside down.

A polar bear
doesn't mind
the cold.
It curls up in the
snow for a nap.

Sea otters float
while fast asleep.

Mountain goats rest on a rocky ledge. Does that look comfy to you?

Author: JENNIFER BOVÉ

Question: If you were an animal, what would be your favorite kind of home?

Answer: I would not choose a tree branch (I might fall off). I would not choose a rocky ledge (it would be too hard). But, I would be perfectly comfy sleeping on a soft bed of moss like the bear in this book.

National Wildlife Federation Naturalist: DAVID MIZEJEWSKI

Question: Have you ever spotted an animal sleeping in the wild?

Answer: It's easy to spot sleeping turtles in ponds in the summertime. They climb out of the water onto fallen logs to bask in the sun and also to take a nap.

Illustrator: PARKER JACOBS *(Ranger Rick & Ricky characters)*

Question: When you were a kid, did you ever stay up drawing past bedtime?

Answer: When I was a kid, I did stay up drawing past my bedtime. In fact, it's a thing that I occasionally do as an adult. I have ruined too many pajamas and bed sheets by falling asleep with a pen in my hand.